A Rainbow Shopping Day

Vivian French

Illustrated by
Selina Young

Orion
Children's Books

For little darling, Missy Skye.
Wishing you a lifetime of love
and happiness, with lots of love
from Auntie Lindsay xxxxx

The stories from *A Rainbow Shopping Day* originally appeared in
The Story House first published in Great Britain in 2004
by Orion Children's Books
This edition first published in 2012
by Orion Children's Books
a division of the Orion Publishing Group Ltd
Orion House
5 Upper St Martin's Lane
London WC2H 9EA
An Hachette UK Company

A catalogue record for this book is available
from the British Library

Printed and bound in China

ISBN 978 1 4440 0517 2

www.orionbooks.co.uk

Contents

A Rainbow Shopping Day

Jason wasn't well. He was still in bed, even though it was nearly lunchtime. Hunter the dog came to sit beside him.

"Woof?" said Hunter.

"I can't play with you today," Jason told him. "I'm not very well."

Mum came into Jason's room. "How are you feeling?" she asked.

Jason sighed. "My head hurts."

"Poor Jason," said Mum. She sat down beside him. "Shall I tell you a story?"

"A story about me?" Jason asked.

"You, and all of us," Mum said.

Jason nodded. "OK."

A Rainbow Shopping Day

It was a Tuesday morning.

"My shoes hurt," said Jason.

"We'll have a look in the market," Mum said. "It's market day today."

"Can I have blue trainers?"
Jason asked.

Mum smiled. "We'll see what
we can find."

They were just about to go
when Granny Annie came
hurrying towards them.

"Where are you off to?"
she asked.

"We're going to the market,"
said Jason. "We're going to buy
blue trainers."

"That's nice," said Granny
Annie. "I'd like to buy a bright red
jumper. I'll come with you."

Jason and Mum and Granny
Annie went down the road.

They hadn't gone far when
Jason's big brother, Ross, came
running up behind them.

"Wait for me!" he said.
"I want to come! Julius
says they've got great
kites at the toy stall.
I want to buy one!"

"I'm going to buy new blue trainers," said Jason. He looked at Ross. "I could help you choose your kite. You could have a blue one, like my trainers.

"A bright red kite would be fun," said Granny Annie. "It would match my bright red jumper."

"What about a yellow kite?" asked Mum. "A yellow one to match the bananas."

"What bananas?" asked Jason.

"The bananas I'm going to buy at the market," said Mum.

"We need oranges too," said Ross. "And apples."

"OK," said Mum. "I'll get oranges and apples as well."

Jason, Mum, Granny Annie and Ross arrived at the market.

"Fruit stall first," said Mum.

They went to the fruit stall, and Mum bought bananas and oranges and apples.

They went to
the wool shop, and
Granny Annie bought
a bright red jumper.

"I want to get my
kite now," said Ross.

They went to the
toy shop.

"Wow!" said
Jason. "Look
at the kites!
Look at all
the colours!"

"Hello!" said a voice, and there was Julius, Jason's step-dad. He and Daisy were looking at the toys too.

"Look!" said Daisy B. "Look at my pink basket!"

"That's lovely," said Mum.

Daisy B smiled. "It's a very lovely basket. Where's Jason?"

Everyone looked round. Jason wasn't there.

"Quick!" said Mum. "Everybody look for him!"

Mum, Granny Annie, Ross, Julius and Daisy B ran to see if Jason was looking at the fruit.

He wasn't there.

They rushed round the corner to the wool shop.

He wasn't there.

They hurried to the market café
in case he'd felt hungry.

He wasn't there.

"Oh! I know where he is!"
said Ross.

He dashed off towards the shoe
stall.

Mum, Granny Annie, Julius and
Daisy B dashed after him – and
there was Jason.

"Hello," he said. "I got bored. Look! They've got blue trainers!"

"Jason!" said Mum as she hugged him. "You must never go off on your own! I thought we'd lost you!"

"Sorry," said Jason. "Can we buy my trainers now?"

"I don't know if you deserve new shoes," Mum said, but she was smiling.

"**Please!**" said Jason. "I promise I won't go off on my own again.

Mum laughed. "All right, Jason. You can have your trainers."

They bought Jason's new blue trainers.

"Well done," said Granny Annie. "Now, let's go and have a cup of tea!"

"I'm worn out," said Mum. "Still, at least we've got everything."

"No, we haven't," said Ross. "I haven't got my kite!"

"Oh, Ross!" said Mum. "I'm too tired to go to the toy shop now!"

"It's OK," Ross said. "I can go on my own."

"I want you to buy a blue kite," Jason said. "Blue to match my trainers!"

"Or a red one to match my jumper," said Granny Annie.

"Pink," said Daisy B. "Like my basket!"

"Yellow," said Mum. "Yellow as a banana."

Julius took the bag of oranges out of Mum's shopping bag. "Orange!"

Mum held up an apple. "What about green?"

"It's my pocket money," Ross said. "I'll choose what colour it is!" And he ran off.

Five minutes later he was back with his brand new kite. It wasn't a **blue** or a **red** or a **pink** or a **yellow** or an **orange** or a **green** kite. It was black with silver stars, but the tail was all the colours of the rainbow.

Granny Annie came to watch. "How lovely!" she said. "A rainbow kite for a rainbow shopping day! The perfect choice."

"I remember that kite," said Jason.
"It got stuck in a tree."

He sat up in bed. "Can you tell
me another story?"

"Just one more," said Mum.
"Then it's lunchtime."

Jason shook his head. "I don't
want any lunch."

"Shall I take Hunter away?"
Mum asked. "You could have a
little sleep."

Jason scratched Hunter's ears.
"I'm not **that** ill. Can you tell me
a story about Hunter?"

Hunter wagged his tail.
"Woof!"

Mum laughed. "He wants to hear the story of how he caught the burglars. You were a hero, weren't you, Hunter?"

Jason grinned. "A hero who was looking for his bone."

"What?" Mum looked surprised. "What was that?"

"I've had a brilliant idea." Jason sat up straighter. "Why don't I tell you the story?"

"Woof!" said Hunter.

Hunter's Lost Bone

Once there was a dog called
Hunter.

He lived in a big house with lots
of children, and two cats.

Hunter liked playing with the children, but he loved playing with his bone.

He liked to bury it in the garden, and dig it up again.

Then one day he lost it.

"Woof!" said Hunter. "Did I bury my bone under the rose bush?"

Hunter dug a big hole under the rose bush, but his bone wasn't there.

"Woof!" he said. "Did I bury it under those blue flowers?"

Hunter dug a bigger hole in the middle of the blue flowers.

His bone wasn't there.

"Woof!" he said. "I know! I buried my bone under those little green leaves!"

Hunter dug a huge hole in the middle of the little green leaves.

His bone wasn't there.

Hunter sat down and scratched his ear. "That's strange," he said. "Where can my bone be?"

"Hunter!" Mum was shouting very loudly. She had come out of the house and seen the holes.

"You are a very bad dog! Just look at my garden! It looks dreadful! My poor poor plants..."

Hunter did his best to look sorry. He hadn't meant to spoil the garden.

"Go into the house!" Mum was still shouting. "You are never to come in the garden again!"

Hunter went slowly into the house. He was very sad. He liked playing ball with Ross and Jason. He liked chasing next door's cat.

When the sun was hot he liked
lying under the apple tree.

It was a lovely garden, and he
would miss it ... and now he would
never find his bone.

That night Hunter had to sleep
in the kitchen.

Mum said he was a bad dog,
and he had to learn not to dig
holes. Hunter wagged his tail to
say he was sorry, but Mum didn't
understand.

Jason was sad too. "Please can Hunter sleep on my bed?" he asked.

Mum still said no.

She put Hunter in the kitchen, and she shut the door.

Hunter couldn't get to sleep.
The cats came in through the cat
flap, and they laughed at him.

"What a bad dog!" they said.

Hunter curled up in a ball, and didn't answer.

It was very late when Hunter heard a noise. He opened his eyes. What was it?

The back door opened.
A torch flashed.
Two men came creeping
into the kitchen.

Hunter sat up, and the men
froze.

"There's a dog!" said one.

Hunter wagged his tail.

"The dog won't stop us," said
the first man. "Let's get that TV."

The two men crept past Hunter, and into the hallway.

Hunter turned round. He was going to go back to sleep, but then he saw the door to the garden was open.

"Woof!" Hunter sat up.

He had had a wonderful idea.
He could look for his bone!

Hunter zoomed out of the door.

There were two scooters
outside. Hunter didn't see them.
He ran straight into them.

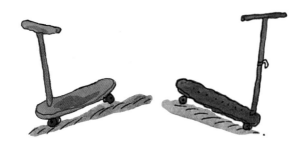

Crash!

The scooters fell over.

"Wowl!" howled Hunter, and
he rushed back into the kitchen ...
just as the men came running out.

Thump! Thump!

The men dashed outside.

Mum came running into the kitchen.

"What's going on?" she asked.

"It's burglars!" Mum shouted. "I'll phone the police!"

"Ouch! Ow! Ouch!"

There was a loud wailing noise from the garden.

"My leg! My leg!" wailed one voice.

"My head! My head!" wailed the other.

The burglars had fallen into Hunter's holes.

They had bumps on their heads, and bruises all over. When the police car came they were very happy to be taken away.

Mum and Julius made a huge fuss of Hunter.

"You're a clever dog," they said. "You're a good dog! Good Hunter!"

Hunter wagged his tail.

"You're such a good dog, you can go in the garden tomorrow," said Mum.

Hunter wagged his tail harder than ever. He'd just remembered something.

He was almost sure his bone was under the tall yellow flowers at the end of the garden ...

Tomorrow he'd go and dig his best hole ever.

Mum was laughing. "Oh my goodness! And I always thought Hunter was a hero!"

"Woof!" Hunter wagged his tail.

"He's the best dog in all the world," Jason said, and he got out of bed. "Can I get up now?"

"Do you feel better?" Mum asked.

Jason nodded. "I feel lots better."

"Woof!" said Hunter.

"Would you like some lunch?"
Mum asked.

"Yes please," Jason said. "I'll
have some lunch, and then I'll
play with Hunter."

"Woof woof woof!"
said Hunter.